#1. I am in school or else I am at out of school. What should I do when I don't know the answer to a question that someone asks?

#1. I have many choices:
  In school, I can raise my hand and guess or else I can keep my hand down.
  Out of school, I can guess or not.
  What is my best choice?

#1. If I guess then I show that person who asked a question that I'm trying even if I give the wrong answer! If that person laughs at me, I can laugh with them at myself and enjoy the fun. If that person gets angry at me for making a joke, I can say I am sorry in a serious way.

#1. If someone calls me a name, I can ignore them because they are not perfect and I know things that they don't know. Then I can learn and think about other things to do the next time when I don't know the answer. Sometimes I can be honest and say, "Sorry, I don't know."

#2. Scientists have found that my brain does grow when I ask questions and when I make mistakes.

In a magnified photo of my brain there are tiny long nerve cells called neurons. They look like leafless trees near each other?

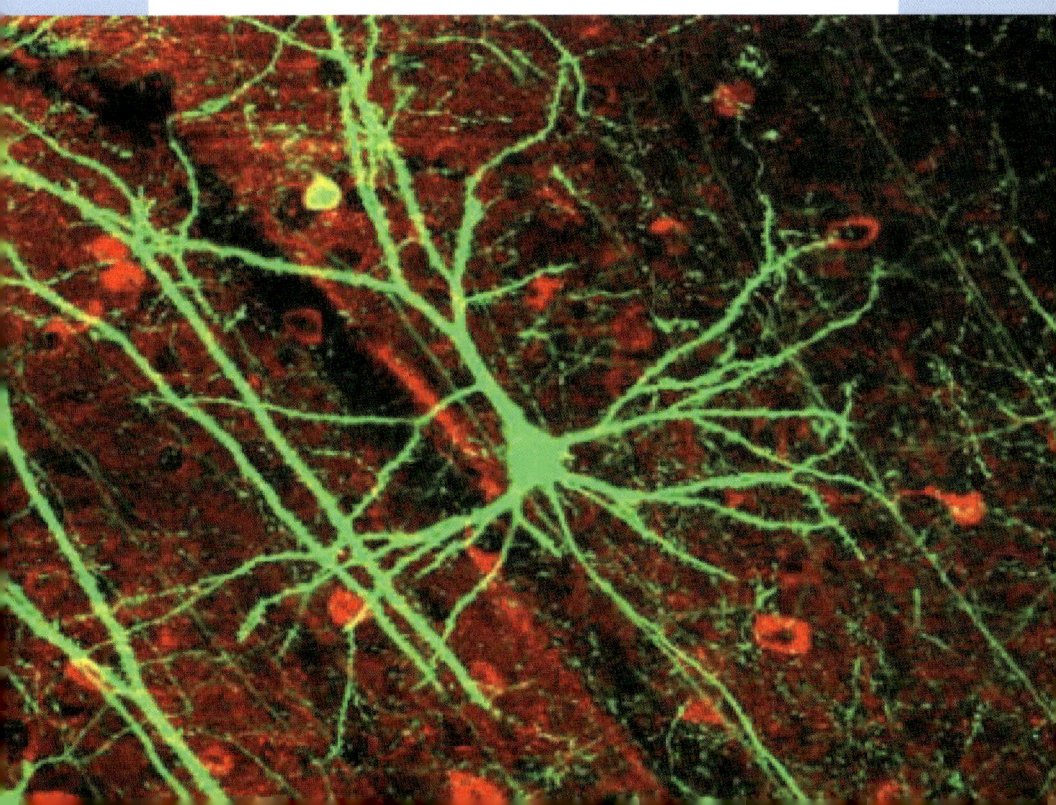

#2. Scientists have found that the number of your brain neurons (nerve cells) increases when you ask questions and when you make mistakes and learn from mistakes!

One neuron sends signals to a second neuron to remember and grow.

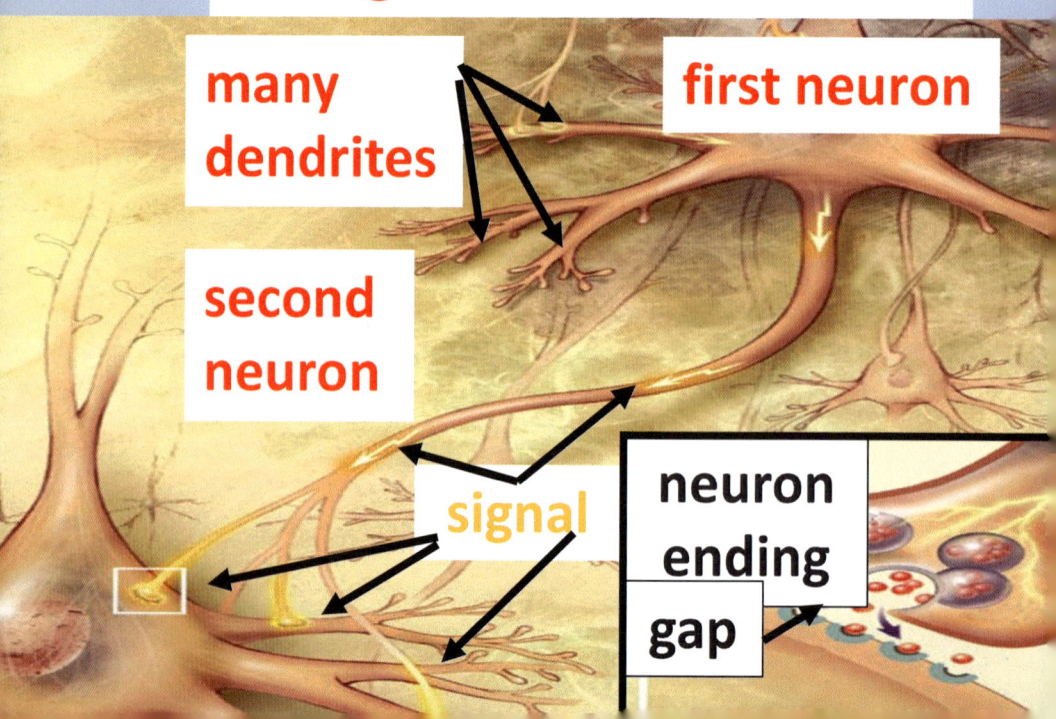

many dendrites

first neuron

second neuron

signal

neuron ending

gap

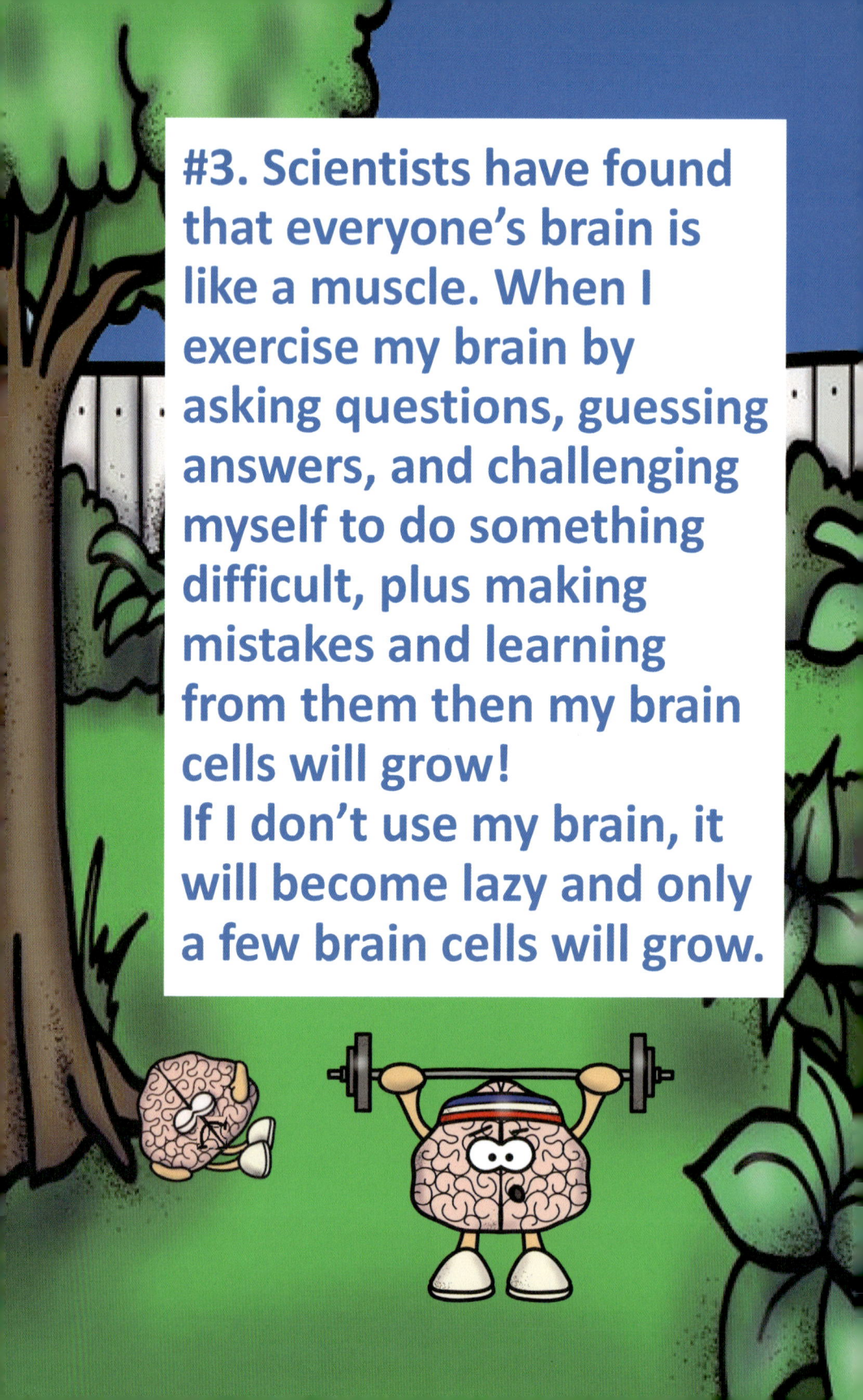

#3. Scientists have found that everyone's brain is like a muscle. When I exercise my brain by asking questions, guessing answers, and challenging myself to do something difficult, plus making mistakes and learning from them then my brain cells will grow!
If I don't use my brain, it will become lazy and only a few brain cells will grow.

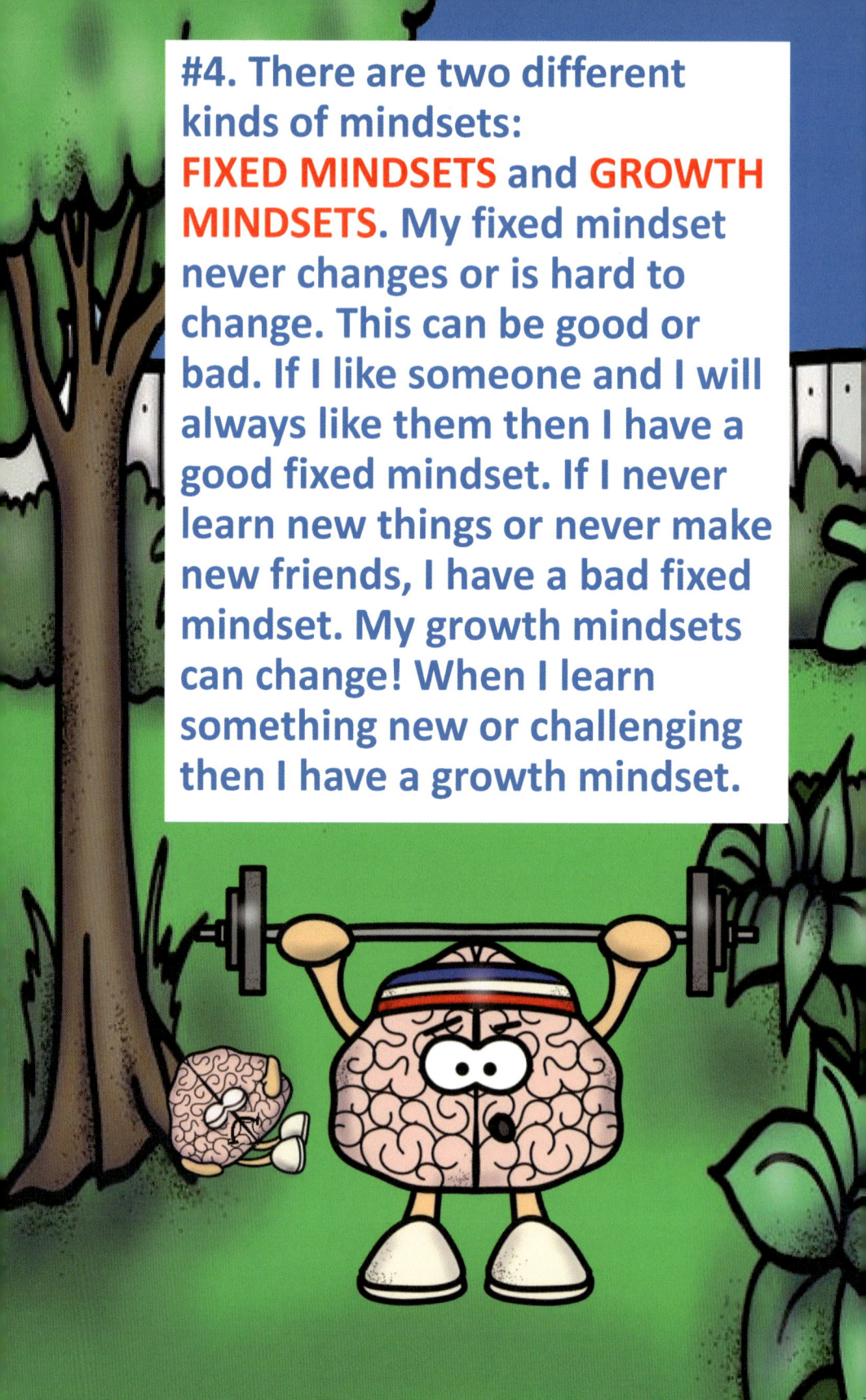

#4. There are two different kinds of mindsets: **FIXED MINDSETS** and **GROWTH MINDSETS**. My fixed mindset never changes or is hard to change. This can be good or bad. If I like someone and I will always like them then I have a good fixed mindset. If I never learn new things or never make new friends, I have a bad fixed mindset. My growth mindsets can change! When I learn something new or challenging then I have a growth mindset.

#5. Can I become smarter?

#5. Scientists have found by experiments that the more you use your brain, the smarter you become. I can become smarter by asking questions even if I know the answer to find out what others think? If I keep reading, listening and challenging myself to focus on learning new things, I can be smarter.

#6. No one is perfect, including me! We all make mistakes! I have to accept mistakes and learn from my own mistakes and the mistakes of others. There's no use crying over spilt milk or past mistakes. I don't get angry when I or other people make mistakes!

#7. It is better to have future plans that I might change than to have no plans. Scientist know that planning and thinking help me learn more in order to make better decisions for myself and for others. Plans can be changed if needed.

#7. I don't want to keep my head always in a cloud. I need to be aware of what's going on around me!
I want to learn from the past, live in the present, and dream and plan for the future!

#8. Can I be whatever I want to be?

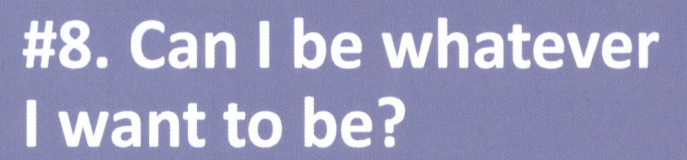

#8. Nobody can do everything they want. Some things are wrong or against the law. On the other hand, scientists have found that sometimes you can achieve what you believe you can achieve. Write down your goals and focus on what you need to do in order to achieve your goals.

#8. Goals can be good or bad for you depending on what you set as goals. If you think you can't do something then you might believe it and never try to do it. **If I think, "I will try to do it and see what happens." Then I have a good chance of doing it! Yet, there are no guarantees. Try again.**

#9. Is laughter really the best medicine?

#9. Scientists have found that laughter can make me healthier and happier. A day without learning and laughing at myself or with others is a day wasted! Be careful not to hurt someone's feelings with a joke.

#9. I am going to buy or check out from the library some humor or joke books. After I find clean jokes that I like, I'll memorize them. I will tell a joke to 10 different people even if they don't laugh or don't get the joke. Now that joke is a part of me and a part of my sense of humor to use in the future!

#10. Which is more important: people and other living things or material things that are not alive?

#10. People and other living things are more important than material things that are not alive. Living things have feelings. Material things do not have feelings.

#11. Even if I'm nervous and have butterflies in my stomach, I can learn to talk better in front of people at school and out of school by practicing in front of a mirror or in front of my parents at home.

#11. I can make faces and use my head, hands, and arms to show emotions like happy, sad, angry, funny, laughing, wonder and so on to be a better speaker. Even the best speakers say that they practice and still get nervous and have butterflies in their stomach.

#12. What is the best way for me to learn and be smarter?

#12. Everybody does not learn the same way! There are at least 4 different ways to learn. One way to learn is by **LISTENING**: Some people learn by listening to someone talking. I learn best by reading out loud or listening to book recordings like those from audiblebooks.com.

#12. I can use a pocket voice recorder in class and listening again to review. It helps if I take oral tests or else I can learn to take written tests by reading "aloud" inside my head. I can easily tell you the words to songs. I usually like to sing or play musical instruments. I'm an auditory or listening learner

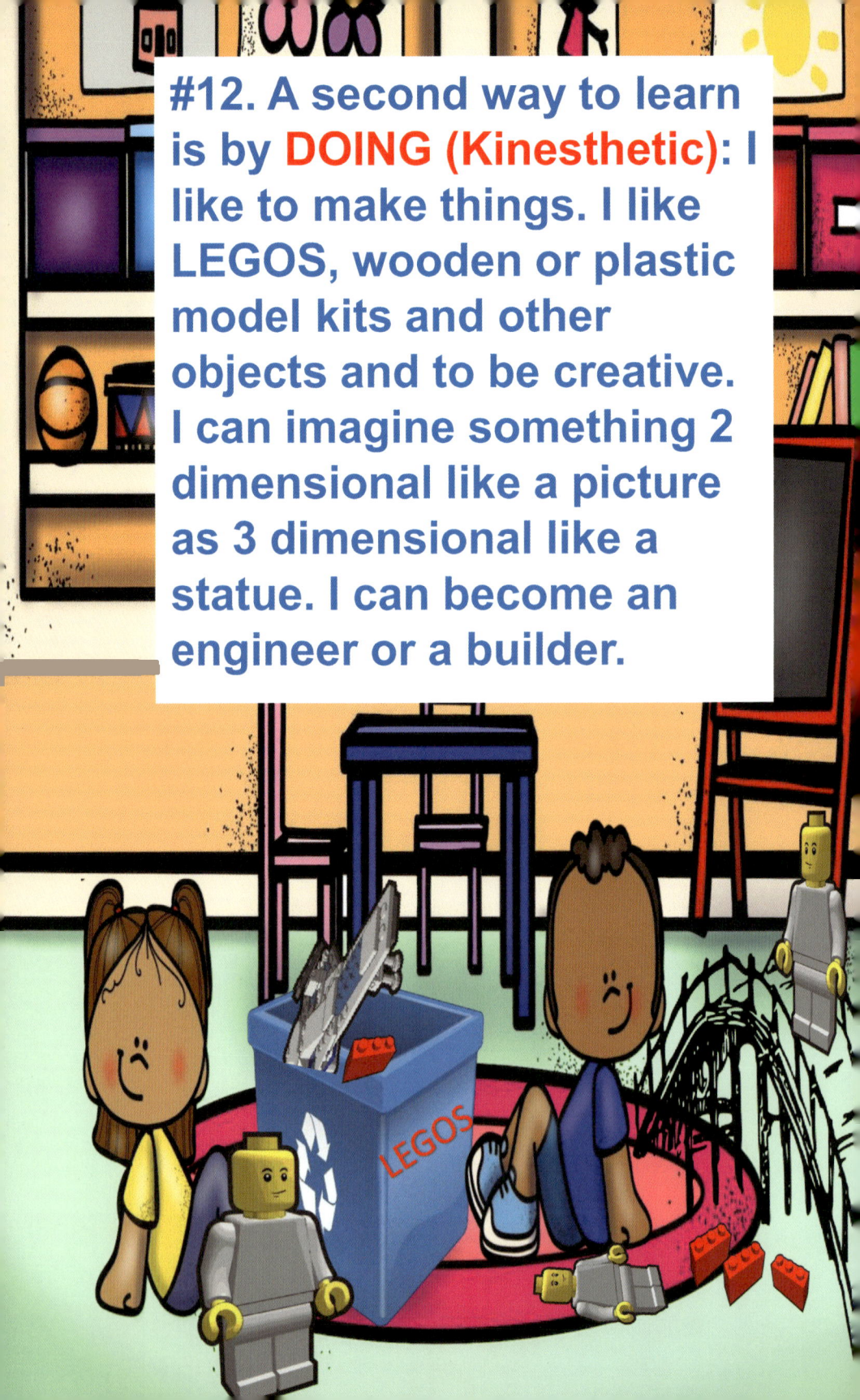

#12. A second way to learn is by **DOING (Kinesthetic)**: I like to make things. I like LEGOS, wooden or plastic model kits and other objects and to be creative. I can imagine something 2 dimensional like a picture as 3 dimensional like a statue. I can become an engineer or a builder.

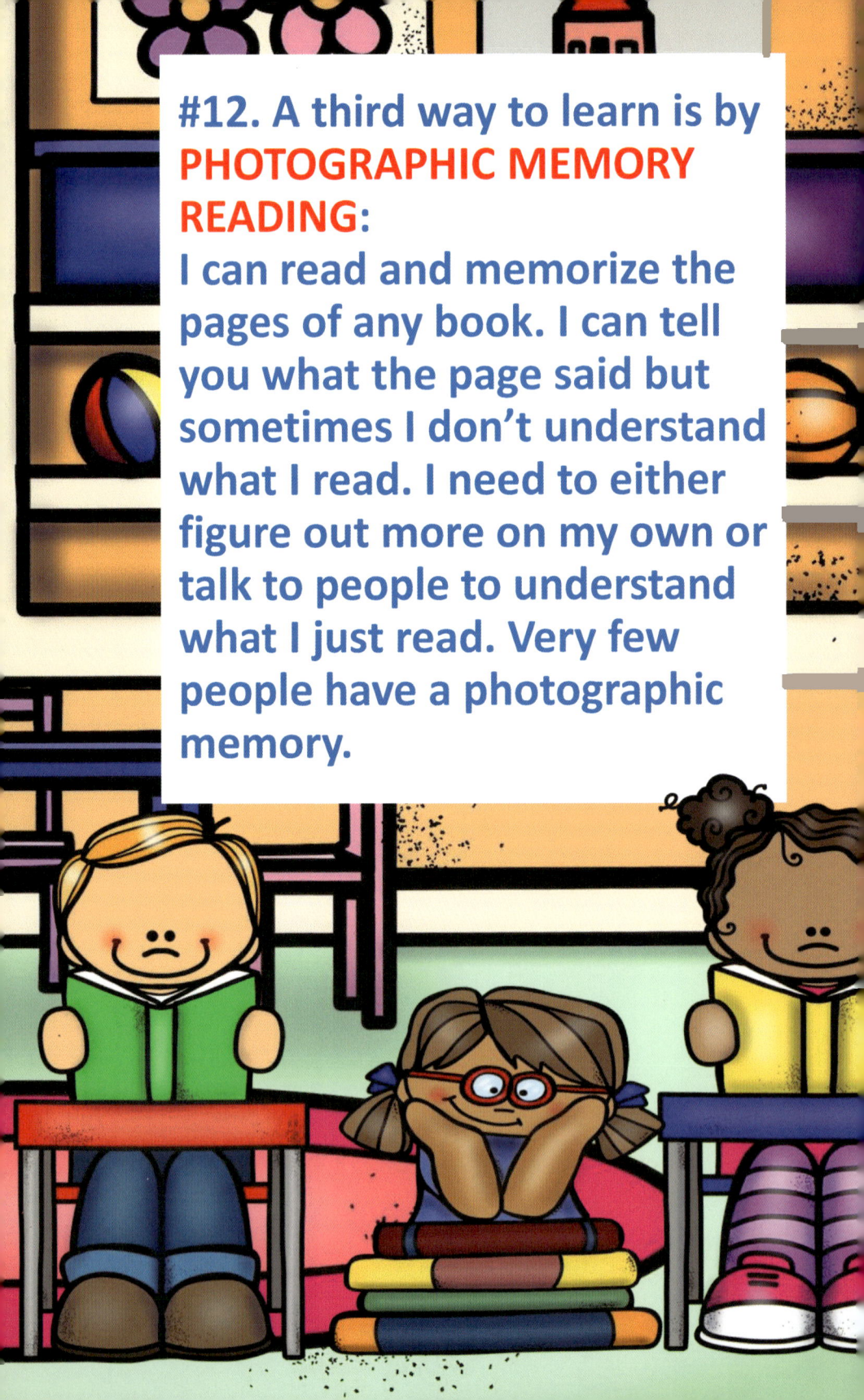

#12. A third way to learn is by **PHOTOGRAPHIC MEMORY READING**: I can read and memorize the pages of any book. I can tell you what the page said but sometimes I don't understand what I read. I need to either figure out more on my own or talk to people to understand what I just read. Very few people have a photographic memory.

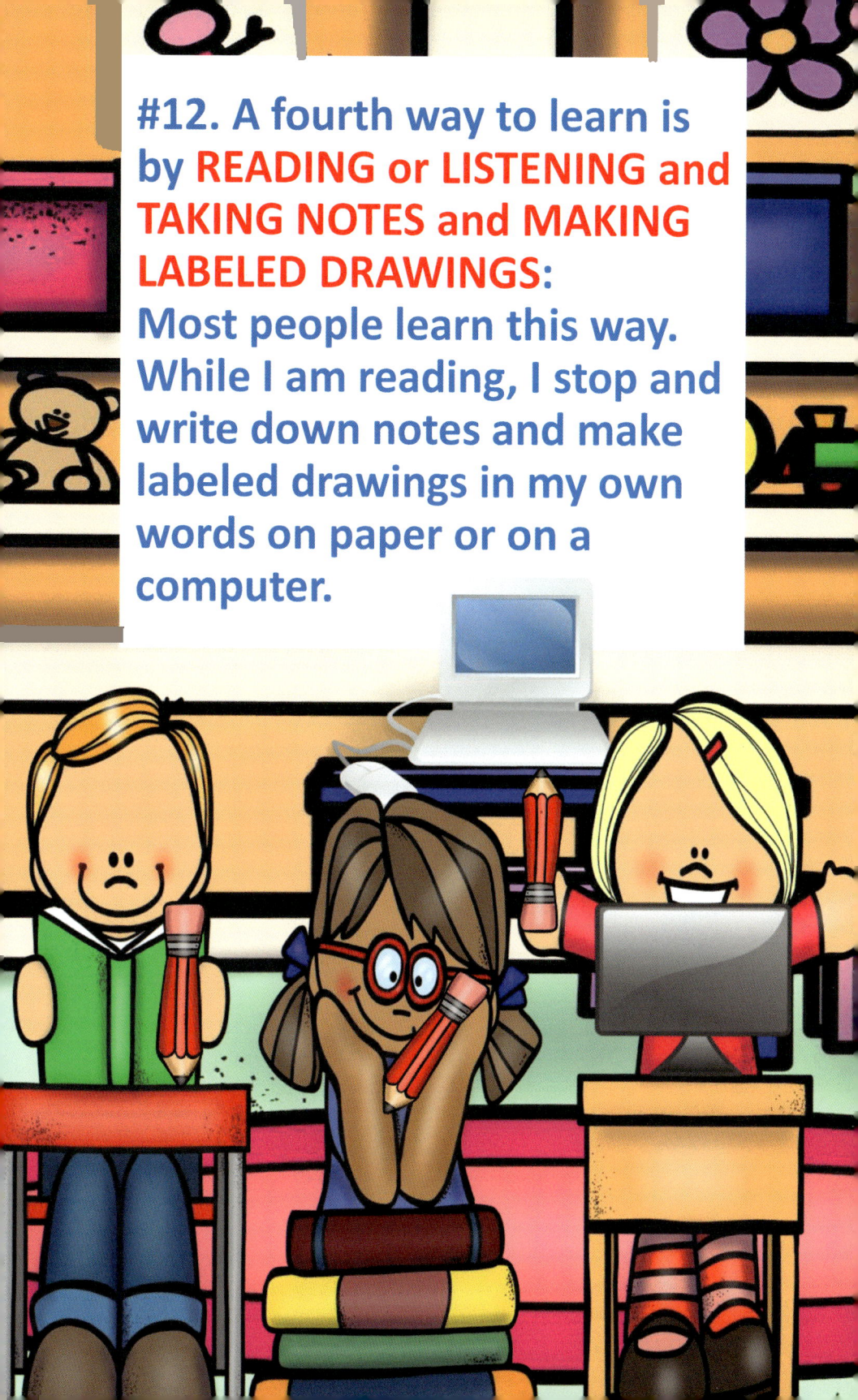

#12. A fourth way to learn is by READING or LISTENING and TAKING NOTES and MAKING LABELED DRAWINGS: Most people learn this way. While I am reading, I stop and write down notes and make labeled drawings in my own words on paper or on a computer.

#12. If I have trouble writing notes, I copy the important words until I learn to write in my own words. Writing my own notes and making my own labeled drawings helps me remember better.

#13. Is money important for me?

#13. Before money was invented, ancient people gathered and hunted for their own food using tools made from stone and wood. They shared or traded for things.

#13. Sea shells, metal coins and paper money were later used to get something. Money is a form of trade. I will get in the habit of saving most of my money for emergencies in the future and each day write down what I spend. I will ask my parents to pay me for chores or do paid chores for people that my parents trust. A lot of money cannot buy happiness. I can be happy with just enough money to get by and enjoy things.

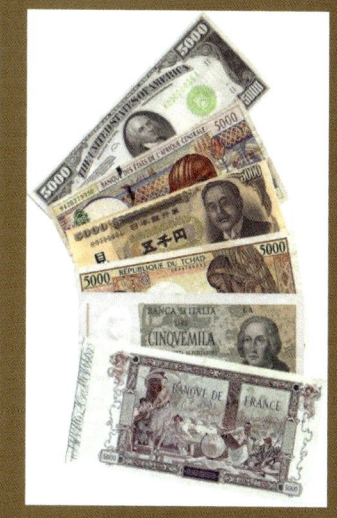

Turn Lose Into Win with Your Words

"I can never do this."
"I haven't yet learned how to do this."
"I never ask for help.
"Please, teach me to how to do this so I can do it by myself."
"I'm embarrassed when I make a mistake."
"I'm not embarrassed when I make mistakes."
"I can never make mistakes."
"Everybody makes mistakes!"
"I never ask questions."
"There's nothing wrong with asking questions."
"I'll never stop until I get it."
"Maybe if I take a break and think about it, I'll get it later."
"I can't do it."
"I will do my best."

Turn Lose Into Win with Your Words

"I never win."

"Sometimes I win. Sometimes I lose."

"Mistakes make me stupid."

"Mistakes make me smarter!"

"I give up. I can't do it.

"I can try!" or "I'll try it again."

"It's looks hard. I won't try it."

"It's looks easy! I'll try it."

"I'll never do it."

"I think I can do it! At least I'll try."

"Mistakes are bad."

"Mistakes are good to learn from."

"I can't do it."

"I will do my best."

"I'm no good."

"I'm as good as anyone!"

"I never ask for help."

"Can you help me, please?"

Turn Lose Into Win with Your Words

"I never learn. I never laugh."

"A day without laughter and learning something new, is a day wasted."

"I quit. I give up."

"I'm not a quitter. I keep trying."

"I'll never be able to do it by myself."

"Please give me some time to try and do it by myself. If I can't do it, I'll ask for help."

"I worry about everything."

"I don't sweat the small things and everything is small things!"

"I don't want to practice. Practice is boring."

"Practice makes me almost perfect. I challenge myself to do my best during practice. I make practice fun."

Note to kids, parents, teachers, counselors, and other adults:

If only one person is reading this book, try to guess before go on. It's okay to be wrong. You can learn from your mistakes.

If two or more persons are reading this book, you might take turns reading the question aloud and have the others guess by writing their answer or saying out loud what it means before going on. It's okay to guess wrong. You can learn from your mistakes and a have good group discussion.

You can use this book as a self-quiz book. Write or say the question number. Then write or say your guess before you go on. Finally, fix any mistakes by saying or writing the answer in your own words.

  Thank you for purchasing this book. Check out my other books. Illustrations purchased from Edu-Clips and from OpenClipArt and Commons Wiki. For over 40 years, I have enjoyed teaching at elementary, high school and college levels. I would love to hear from you. Email me at richardvlinville@gmail.com Dedicated to grandchildren: Mia and Kai as well as anyone who wants to learn about growth mindsets.

"None of us is as smart as all of us."
- Kenneth H. Blanchard

"Grit is about working on something you care about so much that you're willing to stay loyal to it ... It's doing what you love, but not just falling in love – staying in love."
- Angela Duckworth

"So far the best idea I've heard for building grit in kids is something called growth mindset….and it is the belief that the ability to learn is not fixed. That it can change with your effort."
- Angela Duckworth

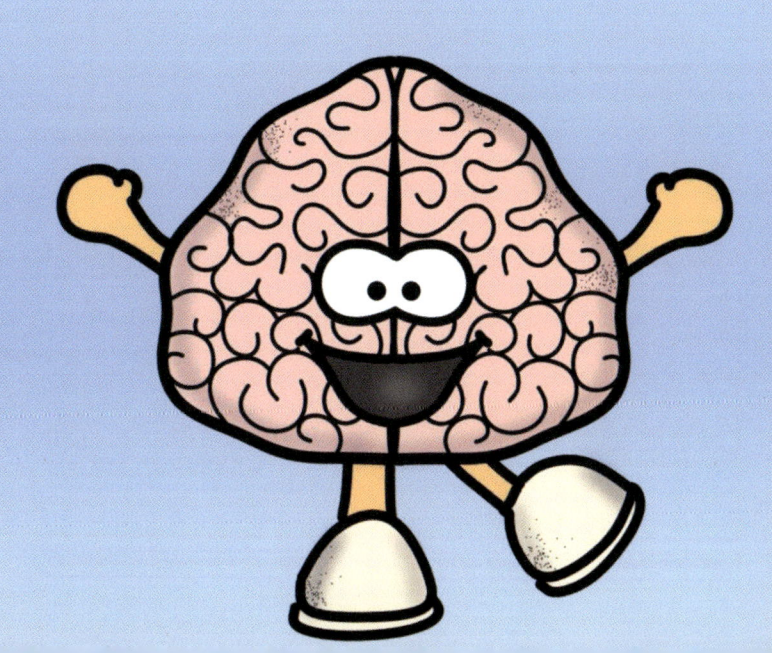

Printed in Great Britain
by Amazon